Don't Lose It— Reuse It!

Nancy Noel Williams

TeachingStrategies™ • Washington D.C.

For Teaching Strategies, Inc.
Publisher: Larry Bram
Editorial Director: Hilary Parrish Nelson
VP Curriculum and Assessment: Cate Heroman
Product Manager: Kai-leé Berke
Book Development Team: Sherrie Rudick and Jan Greenberg
Project Manager: Jo A. Wilson

For Q2AMedia
Editorial Director: Bonnie Dobkin
Editor and Curriculum Adviser: Suzanne Barchers
Program Manager: Gayatri Singh
Creative Director: Simmi Sikka
Project Manager: Santosh Vasudevan
Designer: Ritu Chopra
Picture Researcher: Anita Gill

Picture Credits
t-top b-bottom c-center l-left r-right

Cover: Ariel Skelley/Photolibrary.

Back Cover: Randy Plett/Istockphoto.

Title page: Cathy Yeulet/123RF.

Insides: Mark Bowden/Istockphoto: 3, Banana Stock/ Photolibrary: 4tl, Steven Puetzer/Photolibrary: 4tr, Scrambled/Dreamstime: 4bl, Nick Stubbs/Dreamstime: 4bc, Chris Lowe/Photolibrary: 4br, Ariel Skelley/Photolibrary: 5, Gina Smith/Dreamstime: 6l, Monkey Business Images/ Photolibrary: 6r, Benjamin Gelman/Dreamstime: 7, Bronwyn Photo/Shutterstock: 8, Thomas Perkins/Dreamstime: 9, Photodisc/Photolibrary: 10, Masterfile: 11, Rebecca Emery/ Photolibrary: 12l, Picturephoto/Dreamstime: 12r, FogStock LLC/Photolibrary: 13, Laila Roberg/Istockphoto: 14, Masterfile: 15, Masterfile: 16, Corbis/Photolibrary: 17t, Istockphoto: 17b, Stephen Lynch/Shutterstock: 18, SW Productions/Photolibrary: 19, Jupiterimages/Photolibrary: 20, Julian Winslow/Photolibrary: 21t, Feng Yu/Dreamstime: 21b, Anastasiya Maksimenko/123RF: 22t, Stephanie Phillips/ Istockphoto: 22b, Rmarmion/Dreamstime: 23, Randy Plett/ Istockphoto: 24.

Teaching Strategies, Inc.
P.O. Box 42243
Washington, DC 20015
www.TeachingStrategies.com

ISBN: 978-1-60617-134-9

Library of Congress Cataloging-in-Publication Data
Williams, Nancy Noel.
  Don't lose it—reuse it! / Nancy Noel Williams.
    p. cm.
  ISBN 978-1-60617-134-9
  1. Recycling (Waste, etc.)--Juvenile literature. 2. Waste minimization--Juvenile literature.
  3. Handicraft--Juvenile literature. I. Title.
  TD794.5.W495 2010
  745.58'4--dc22
                    2009036782

CPSIA tracking label information:
RR Donnelley, Shenzhen, China
Date of Production: March 2012
Cohort: Batch 2

Printed and bound in China

3 4 5 6 7 8 9 10	15 14 13 12
Printing	Year Printed

Every day we throw things away.

But before you toss
something into the trash...

Stop!

Think!

Recycle!

Ask yourself:
How can I reuse this?

RECYCLE

What can you make with cardboard tubes?

Make a telescope or play on your horn.

Cut some tubes in half.
Decorate each one
to make napkin rings.

Make a tunnel
for your race car.

Decorate some tubes and boxes
to make your very own robot.

What can you do with old buttons and beads?

String beads together to hang in your room. See how long you can make the string.

Gather some pine cones. Glue colorful
buttons on them to make decorations.

What can you do with big and small boxes?

Put a gift in a box. You can decorate some paper. Then wrap up the box.

Make a tower by piling the boxes up.

What can you do with really big boxes?

Cut out windows and
make your own playhouse.

If you have a marker and a box,
you can make your own race car.

Zoom! Zoom!

What can you make with paper bags?

Don't throw away that lunch bag.

Draw a funny face on a paper bag. You have made a hand puppet.

Make a larger puppet with a grocery bag.
Have a puppet show with your friends.

What can you make with old newspapers?

Fold the newspapers into boats.

Make some hats to wear with a friend.

What can you do with old clothes?

Use hats, shoes, and old jewelry to make a costume. Change your voice and your name. Become a new character!

Grab some
kitchen things
and have
a parade.

An old shirt makes
a great paint smock.

17

What can you do with sticks and sponges?

Make your own group of wacky stick people.

Make a painting with sponges.

What can you make with empty bottles and cans?

Wash out a bottle. Cut an opening, like an open door, on its side. Put bird seeds inside. Hang the bottle in a tree and watch the birds eat.

Fill cans with dirt and plant flower or vegetable seeds. Water the seeds and watch them grow.

Keep your pencils organized in an empty can.

What can you make with socks?

Find some buttons
and thread for eyes.

Sew some yarn on
for hair. You have
made a sock puppet.

Write a story and act it out.

Don't lose your chance to make
something new the next time
you pick up some trash.

Take a good look. Then
remember—don't lose it.
Reuse it!